ELECTRIFIED!

WHAT IS A CIRCUIT?

Gareth Stevens
Publishing

By Ethan Weingarten

Please visit our website, www.garethstevens.com. For a free color catalog of all our high-quality books, call toll free 1-800-542-2595 or fax 1-877-542-2596.

Library of Congress Cataloging-in-Publication Data

Weingarten, Ethan
    What is a circuit? / by Ethan Weingarten.
cm. – (Electrified!)
Includes bibliographical references and index.
Summary: This book explains how electric circuits work, describes different
types of electric circuits, and tells how resistors and transistors control the flow of current.
Contents: Shocking science – Popping electrons – Round and round – Three-part
path – The switch – Series circuit – Parallel circuit – Short circuit – Resistors and transistors.
ISBN 978-1-4339-8415-0 (pbk.)
ISBN 978-1-4339-8416-7 (6-pack)
ISBN 978-1-4339-8414-3 (hard bound)
    1. Electric circuits—Juvenile literature   2. Electricity—Juvenile literature
[1. Electricity]   I. Title
                2013
        621.319—dc23

First Edition

Published in 2013 by
Gareth Stevens Publishing
111 East 14th Street, Suite 349
New York, NY 10003

Copyright © 2013 Gareth Stevens Publishing

Designer: Katelyn E. Reynolds
Editor: Therese Shea

Photo credits: Cover, p. 1 limpido/Shutterstock.com; cover, pp. 1 (logo), 11, 15, 21 iStockphoto/Thinkstock.com; cover, pp. 1, 3–24 (background) Lukas Radavicius/Shutterstock.com; cover, pp. 1, 3–24 (image frame) VikaSuh/Shutterstock.com; p. 5 Martin Poole/Lifesize/Thinkstock.com; p. 7 Hemera/Thinkstock.com; p. 9 Image Source/Getty Images; pp. 13, 17 Dorling Kindersley RF/Thinkstock.com; p. 19 Thomas Skjaeveland/Shutterstock.com.

Printed in the United States of America

CPSIA compliance information: Batch #CW13GS: For further information contact Gareth Stevens, New York, New York at 1-800-542-2595.

CONTENTS

Words in the glossary appear in **bold** type the first time they are used in the text.

SHOCKING SCIENCE

When you were young, your parents probably told you to stay away from electrical outlets. They didn't want you to get **electrocuted**. Now you know there's electricity in there, just waiting to get out. That electricity needs a path—and you don't want it to be you!

The path through which electricity flows is called a circuit. A circuit needs to be set up in a certain way to provide power, or energy, for our electrical **devices**. The more you learn about circuits, the more you understand how electrical devices work.

When people are electrocuted, they're part of a path of electricity. This can be very dangerous and even deadly. Always be careful around electrical outlets and wires.

POPPING ELECTRONS

An atom is a building block of matter. An electron is a tiny **particle** that circles the center of an atom. Electrons can pop off one atom and jump to another. Electricity is the free flow of electrons from one atom to another.

Some atoms lose and gain electrons more easily than others. Conductors are materials made up of atoms like these. Electrical circuits must be made of conductors so electricity can pass easily through them.

POWER FACT!

Electrons don't flow well through materials called insulators. Atoms in these materials hold on to their electrons.

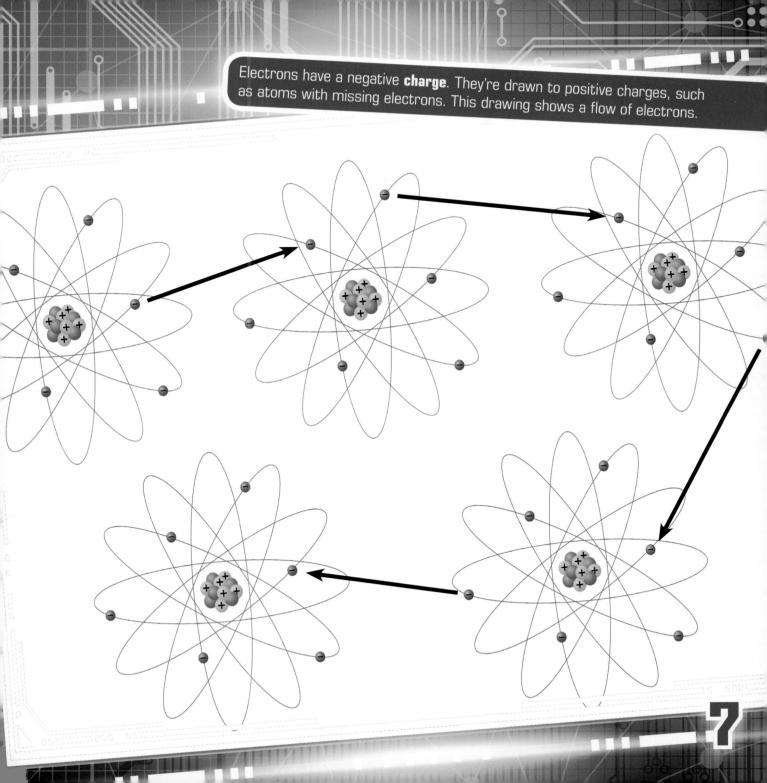

Electrons have a negative **charge**. They're drawn to positive charges, such as atoms with missing electrons. This drawing shows a flow of electrons.

ROUND AND ROUND

Electrical circuits must begin and end at the same point, forming a kind of loop. Imagine you have a robot that can move with the help of a **battery**. A circuit provides a path for the battery's energy. When you place the battery in the robot, electricity flows into the wires inside the robot, which are conductors.

As electricity flows, the robot moves. The electricity then travels back to the battery. If it didn't return to the energy source, the electrons would stop flowing.

POWER FACT!

The flow of electricity is called a current.

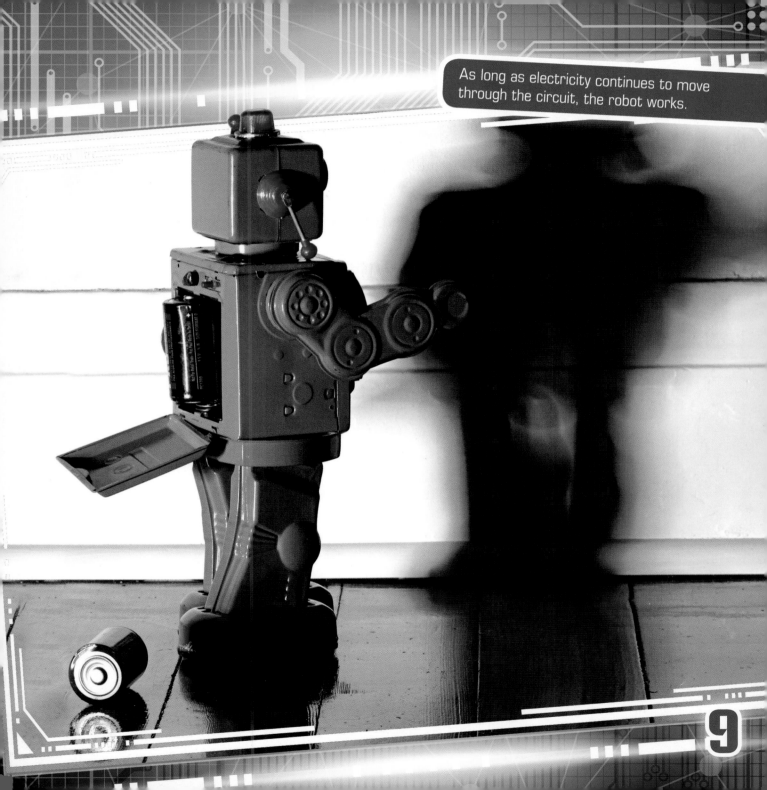

As long as electricity continues to move through the circuit, the robot works.

THREE-PART PATH

All circuits have at least three parts:

- The energy source is where electricity comes from, such as a battery or **generator**.

- The load is the object that needs electrical power. It's also called an output device.

- The conductive path is the way the electrical current flows.

In your robot, the energy source is the battery. The load is the robot's parts, and the conductive path is made up of the wires that run through the parts.

An outlet isn't an energy source. The actual source is probably a power plant generator. It makes electricity that flows through power lines to your home's outlets.

11

THE SWITCH

Your robot probably doesn't just move until the battery runs out of energy. It most likely has a **switch** or button to turn it on and off.

A switch is an easy way to interrupt the flow of current through a circuit. When the switch is in the off position, there's a gap in the path. The electrons can't jump the gap. This is called an open circuit. When the switch is turned on, there are no gaps and electricity flows. This is called a closed circuit.

POWER FACT!

If electrical devices didn't have switches, we'd have to remove batteries or unplug the devices from the energy source to stop them.

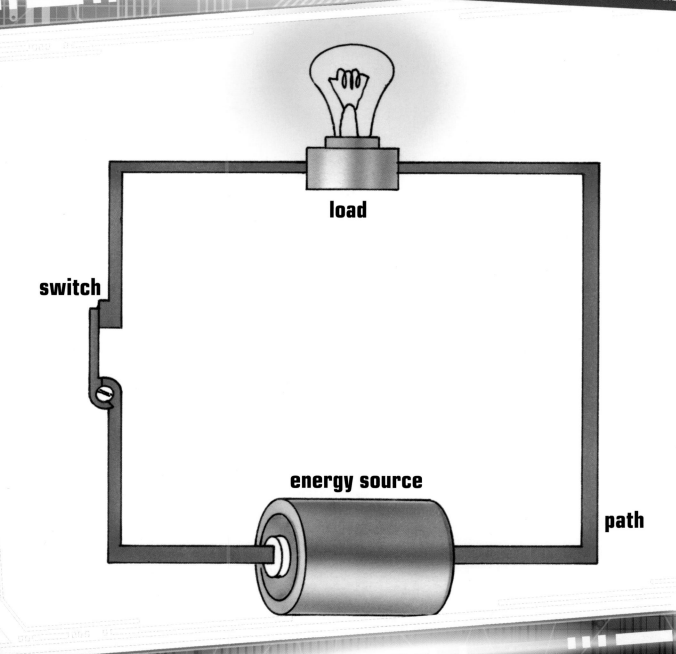

load

switch

energy source

path

SERIES CIRCUIT

A series circuit is a single path through which current flows. If one part of the path is broken, the circuit won't work. Some holiday lights are an example of a series circuit. If one bulb won't light, the circuit is broken and none of the bulbs can receive energy.

Series circuits are simple, but they're not always the best way to make a circuit. Imagine if your TV went off every time a lightbulb burned out. If these devices were powered by the same series circuit, that might happen!

POWER FACT!

Current is measured in units called amperes, or amps. One amp is a flow of 6,250,000,000,000,000,000 electrons per second! That's 6.25 quintillion electrons!

You'd have to replace a broken bulb in these holiday lights to make the series circuit work again.

15

PARALLEL CIRCUIT

Parallel circuits provide more than one path through which current can flow. However, all parallel circuits have a single path back to the source. Each parallel path is called a branch. If a branch breaks, the electricity still flows because there are more branches to follow.

Homes are wired with parallel circuits. Each branch receives the same amount of current. This way, the many loads in a home—such as lights, computers, TVs, and appliances—can operate separately.

All circuits, series and parallel, carry the current in one direction. This is an example of a parallel circuit.

load

load

energy source

SHORT CIRCUIT

Parallel circuits can have problems. A short circuit happens when a path is **bypassed** in some way. For example, two broken wires may touch. The current keeps flowing since the circuit has no gaps and is still closed.

However, it's possible for too much current to flow through the circuit. Too much current means wires can heat up and may even start a fire. Houses have **fuses** or circuit breakers that shut down circuits if this happens.

POWER FACT!

Too much current can break the devices receiving electricity.

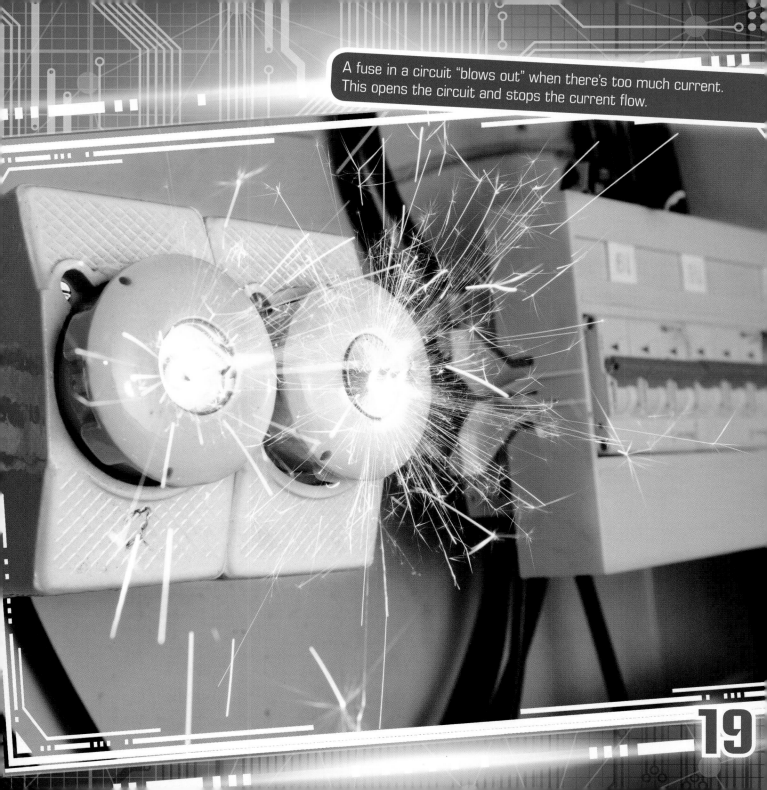

A fuse in a circuit "blows out" when there's too much current. This opens the circuit and stops the current flow.

19

RESISTORS AND TRANSISTORS

A resistor is a device that's placed in a circuit to control current. Resistors resist, or oppose, a certain amount of electricity. Not all loads use the same amount of electrical energy. Resistors help them receive the amount they need.

Transistors can switch current on and off, and even strengthen the current in a circuit. Transistors are key parts of almost all electronic devices, including cell phones and computers. We wouldn't have either of these devices without resistors, transistors, and circuits!

POWER FACT!

Your body can be a conductor. That's why it's important not to touch live electrical wires.

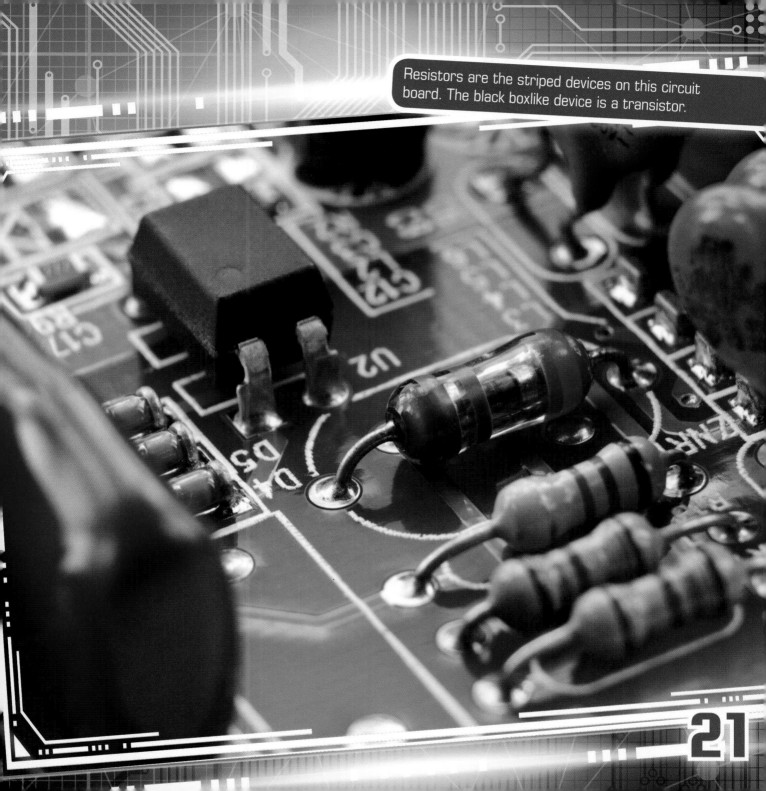

Resistors are the striped devices on this circuit board. The black boxlike device is a transistor.

GLOSSARY

battery: a device that turns chemical energy into electricity

bypass: to avoid a place by traveling around it

charge: an amount of electricity

device: a tool or machine made to perform a task

electrocute: to cause injury or death by electricity

fuse: an electrical safety device with a piece of metal that melts if the current running through it passes a certain level

generator: a machine that uses moving parts to produce electrical energy

parallel: describing lines that are the same distance apart at all points

particle: a very small piece of something

switch: a device that opens, closes, or changes the connections in an electrical circuit

FOR MORE INFORMATION

Books

Monroe, Ronald. *What Are Electrical Circuits?* New York, NY: Crabtree Publishing, 2012.

Oxlade, Chris. *Making a Circuit.* Chicago, IL: Heinemann Library, 2012.

Richardson, Adele. *Electricity: A Question and Answer Book.* Mankato, MN: Capstone Press, 2006.

Websites

Electricity: How Circuits Work
www.hantsfire.gov.uk/circuits
Watch a simple video about circuits.

Electricity Teaching Resources
www.woodlands-junior.kent.sch.uk/revision/science/electricity.htm
Find many links to electricity websites and quizzes.

INDEX